BECOMING THE BLUE HERON

Also by Terri Kirby Erickson

Thread Count
Telling Tales of Dusk
In the Palms of Angels
A Lake of Light and Clouds

Becoming the Blue Heron

Poems

Terri Kirby Erickson

Press 53
Winston-Salem

Press 53, LLC

PO Box 30314

Winston-Salem, NC 27130

First Edition

Cover design by Kevin Morgan Watson

Cover art, "Untitled," Copyright © 2015 by Stephen White

Author portrait Copyright © 2014 by Lynne Srba

Printed on acid-free paper

ISBN 978-1-941209-53-0

for Mother and Daddy,
my best friends

Many thanks to the editors of the following publications where these poems or versions of them first appeared:

Annals of Internal Medicine: "COPD," Ann Intern Med. *2016* Nov 1;*165(9):672*, ©American College of Physicians

Asheville Poetry Review Anniversary Issue: "Pearl," "You"

Atlanta Review: "Lightning Bugs"

BoomerLitMag: "Nostalgia"

Bop Dead City: "My Cousin, Milton"

Broad River Review: "Pixie Cut"

Connotation Press: "Pilar Rioja Dancing in Neil Goldberg's Studio," "Tahara"

Cutthroat, A Journal of the Arts: "After the Explosion"

Dappled Things: "Rosemary, Riding"

Das Literarisch: "Jacqueline with Flowers," "The Street Walker"

Eunoia Review: "Gulls"

Garo: "Black Vultures"

Glass Lyre Press Collateral Damage (Anthology): "The Cost of War"

Iodine: "Caballero," "Spider in the Sink," "Valerie"

Kakalak 2015: "Suppertime"

Kakalak 2016: "Granny, Dragged by a Cow"

MockingHeart Review: "Family Album," "The Abortion," "Red Lion"

NASA (National Aeronautics and Space Administration) History Program Office News & Notes, Volume 33, Number 2: "Moon Walk"

O.Henry Magazine: "Sheller," "Blue Jays," "The Gray and the Brown," "When Honey Bees Were Everywhere," "Winter"

Old Mountain Press: "Dressing Room Blues"

Pinesong: "Bloom"

Salt Magazine: "Sheller"

The Ofi Press: "Angel"

Award-Winning Poems:

Publication Prize Winner, 2016 Atlanta Review
   International Poetry Competition, "Lightning Bugs"
Finalist, 2015 Ron Rash Award (*Broad River Review*), "Pixie
   Cut"
Winner, 2014 Joy Harjo Poetry Prize (*Cutthroat*), "After the
   Explosion"
Finalist, 2014 Randall Jarrell Poetry Competition, "Tahara"
Second Place, 2014 Poetry of Courage Award, North
   Carolina Poetry Society (*Pinesong*), "Bloom"

Becoming the Blue Heron

INTRODUCTION

Full disclosure: Terri Kirby Erickson is a dear friend. That means that writing about her poems is both a pleasure and a challenge because I worry that you, dear readers, will think I am biased. Trust me for a bit as I try to fuse the personal and the critical to invite you into these poems in *Becoming the Blue Heron*, a book that features both the best of what Terri has done before alongside an even deeper delving into subjects that her unbiased eye and fine craft reveal with heart.

Terri entered my life when we heard each other read our poems in 2009 at Poetry Hickory, a reading series coordinated by poet Scott Owens, not long after *Telling Tales of Dusk* came out. At this reading, Terri sat in the back of the Taste Full Beans at a small table with her husband Leonard, her most devoted fan (see "The Oceanic" for a scene with him at another table). Hearing her for the first time, I was struck by the frank clarity of her poems. Terri and I then met in passing, the way poets sharing a stage can do. But Terri has an awesome memory for details, one that serves her well in poetry and in friendship. Months later, she remembered meeting me when she came to the college where I work.

In September of 2010, Henry McCarthy, host of "Poets and Writers," was to interview Terri for the WEHC radio series he has hosted for years through the public radio station of Emory & Henry College. (You can find an archival audio copy via www.ehc.edu, and the full CD archive is also available in the Henry McCarthy Collection of the Southern Folklife Collection of the University of North Carolina at Chapel Hill. Preparing to write this introduction, in fact, I listened again to this broadcast.) During arrangements for the interview, Terri mentioned to Henry that she had met a poet who worked at Emory & Henry College. Henry emailed me to come over to say "hi" before the interview.

After the interview, I was invited to join Henry and his wife Patti along with the Ericksons at Harvest Table Restaurant in downtown Meadowview. I will never forget this evening, not only because it provided the backdrop of conversations that were the catalyst for a fast friendship but also because I killed a black rat snake en route to the restaurant. I was rattled by this, however accidental, by the time I got to the restaurant, wondering if I should be going out to supper when I am a reclusive person often likely just to stay home in the face of invitations. Was the sacrifice of a snake worth the effort?

It was. Seeing a black rat snake dead, after killing it, could feel like an omen, especially as this day was the first day I was living anew with a fresh diagnosis of cancer, which may be why I wanted to get out of the house or why I did not see the snake camouflaged on the pavement, or why, most of all, I would be drawn to Terri as a person and a poet; indeed, as a poet who could write a poem like "Murmuration" or "Barn Owl," poems that address how the imagery of stark nature informs our soulful cries of the heart. (Terri understands what it means to see a black snake in the road.)

During the meal and after, Terri and I, as they say, bonded. We then spoke at length in the parking lot of the restaurant, and this exchange included the revelation of news that not even those in my immediate circle knew yet, the news about my cancer. In fact, "Empathy," a poem that would appear in *In the Palms of Angels* (2011) emerged out of that evening. "Empathy" is the sort of poem that lets us see how much can be shared, quickly, through observation or dialogue, which is what Terri's discerning eye does as she lives her poet's life. The intimacy of our exchange during the visit to Emory & Henry set the pace for a growing friendship that, at first, centered around periodic calls from Terri to check on me or coax me through my fears.

Terri is a kind person. Anybody who meets her at the grocery store or a poetry reading or a doctor's office will know this within minutes. Just read "Playing the Slots." That kindness, apart from her poetry and yet an intrinsic part of the way she looks at the world, kept her in my life after what might have been a special evening at Harvest Table was enjoyed and forgotten. Her empathy, her kindness, her experience as a volunteer with Forsyth Cancer Center, helped her to help me during an arduous year that included cancer treatments, a divorce, and not only the death of the black rat snake but also an old friend.

Her own experience with health challenges, about which she has written and spoken publicly, has informed her natural sense of empathy for others. Her ability to talk about all aspects of her own life is infectious. As she said to Henry during her interview, speaking about the Crohn's Disease she has had since fifteen, "I am happy to put a face on a disease that a lot of people are too embarrassed to talk about." Terri is not embarrassed to talk about much, in the way of the southern storyteller that she is, and invites others to feel open and safe through conversation and poetry. She talks about abortion in this new collection in a way that reflects without polemic on a young woman's (the narrator's) choice to terminate a high-risk pregnancy—a choice that allows her to become a mother later in life ("The Abortion").

Terri's poems tell us that nothing is as simple, or as complicated, as it seems.

I know it is a fallacy always to see a poem in the same light as an author's psyche or life, as poems are fictions even when they share truths, but I also believe that poems are expressions of a fascinating brain that fuses the imagination and life experiences, and mesmerizes us with a person's inner workings. This happens with Terri's poems, for me, and I think that it happens for others who come to know her on the page. Consider "Nostalgia," which asserts, "The past is a set of white curtains, a window / nailed shut beyond which everyone // is happy." What I like best about her poems is how her voice resonates with clarity and honesty in a way that might invite the most resistant among us to look at something simple, or something challenging, in a new light, including a rooster or a bee.

I want to say too that I am charmed by Terri's ability to spin a tale, craft a simile, and invent a poetic fiction that tells a deep, personal truth or spins a true story with the detachment of an artist and the depth of an old soul, even when writing about people closest to her. Skip ahead to "COPD," for example, to read, "Listening to my father cough, struggle for breath . . . I want to lasso / / the air, capture it like a runaway calf and give it / to him the way he used to bring home / money." Family remains a central topic in this collection, along with nature, personal experiences, and what I call witnessing. Sometimes all elements come together, as in "Old Photograph."

"Bloom," a poem that Terri initially wrote as a gift to me at a challenging time during my experience with cancer, appears in this collection (and framed in manuscript form above my own writing desk). I think that it also synthesizes what Terri does so well in her poems about nature, family, and people she contemplates on their life's journeys. The poem also exemplifies the sort of character sketch, or poetic story, that Terri does so well. It offers a perceptive reading of an individual with its imagery of hope to balance a narrative of fear. Inserting a tone of lightness into a subject that is deep and dark, the poem becomes more than a pep talk to me alone. It resonates with a story that shows a more boundless hope that can touch others seeing the unnamed subject of the poem.

The poem's use of the third-person pronoun sets off as a character study the woman in the poem, as other poems do with people Terri has observed in life (for example, "Girl Riding a Bicycle, Holding a Blue Umbrella" and "Rosemary, Riding"), or in art ("Pilar Rioja Dancing in Neil Goldberg's Studio"). It brings the subject to life with a promise of spring past a "chill wind." Another feature that we see here, as in so many poems, is the Ericksonian simile (my term for Terri's deft similes that lead us to see connections in interesting ways). Her readers in general believe that Terri's phrasing of similes and related figurative language is one of her exceptional strengths. Here, for example, the unexpected juxtaposition of parts of the poem leads us into new territory with the imagination.

In this case, the "body" as "a house that needs tearing down, a place where no one wants to live / anymore" is reversed with the assertion that "she isn't done with her body, her life." The attention to natural imagery resounds here, as elsewhere, and the conclusion of the poem calls to mind the way so many poems invoke an innocence of easier, or earlier, times. I like it, and it also won Second Place in the 2014 Poetry of Courage Award presented by the North Carolina Poetry Society and was published in *Pinesong*, so I am not alone.

Perception, then, is key, when I think about what Terri does well. She looks carefully at others, people she knows and people she sees as she goes through her life (she does not really know a stranger), and she looks carefully at herself with a frankness that is accessible and engaging at the same time it goes deep. As E. Reid Gilbert said in a reader's review posted on Amazon, "Terri Kirby Erickson is one of the most compelling poets out of the gate in quite a while. Her treatment of people, events and places with such compassion and candor, is refreshing indeed—but never judgment. When she introduces you to the diverse characters on her path, you will meet them on their own terms of reality and endearment." We see this in "Bloom," and we see it in many poems such as "The Street Walker," inspired by Toulouse-Lautrec, and "Pearl," "luminous as lantern."

When *In the Palms of Angels* appeared in 2011, Kathryn Stripling Byer, Poet Laureate of North Carolina, 2005-2009, in her blog *Here, Where I Am* commented on a "quality of quiet attention and recollection" within the poems in that book. We see that here in this new collection, and then some, as if a few more stops have been pulled out, more inhibitions released. Terri still likes writing about home, as she said in her interview with Henry, "homes, in general, how you feel, the warmth and security and safety of that." There is sometimes a tenuous connection between the warmth and security of home and the threat of something—something like cancer or an unrecognized death or a tragic end to a young life—that shows a recognition of the paradoxes of life. "Moon Walk" exemplifies that tenuous connection, as does "Old Photograph."

The fact that Terri's great-grandfather on her mother's side (see "Rail Walking" for a glimpse of him) was both a Primitive Baptist minister and coffin maker almost preordained Terri's fate as a poet who tells stories to make sense of life's sacred and profane mysteries. Some of these poems are poems that lay to rest some memory or scene at the same time we know that so much dwells underneath. "Monteen" and "Granny, Dragged by a Cow," are great examples of Terri's wit in the service of her craft. Then there is Tommy, Terri's brother (1959-1980), whom we first met in *Thread Count* (2006), Terri's first book. He is a presence in so many memories and poems even if we do not see his face. The tradition of southern storytelling that shares family stories does not mince words, as we see in "After the Explosion" (winner of the 2014 Joy Harjo Poetry Prize and published in *Cutthroat: A Journal of the Arts*), a poem that touches on the loss of her brother and the effect on the poet's relationship with themes of security and innocence.

This ability to be vulnerable has been essential for schooling both the poet's voice and her insights. If Wordsworth claimed that poetry "takes its origin from emotion recollected in tranquility," Erickson provides evidence that this "spontaneous overflow of powerful feelings" about which Wordsworth wrote, is balanced by the craft that mediates tranquility and spontaneity. We see that in narrative and lyric poems, in poems about people or trees or God's creatures.

Although I have suggested that it is okay to skip to one poem or the other, and I have drawn your attention to particular poems, the pacing of this collection means that this book can be read front to back. Reading that way, you will find poems that provide prismatic images of nature as signposts. "Merlot Redbud" offers up a whisper that reminds us of how motionless a human body can become, "like a feather lies / still after falling." "Red and White Tulip," "Five Does," and many more poems help us see the sanctity of life within its natural setting, offering a serenity that reflects a light that shines from Terri's poetry, no matter what comes.

When Terri was working on this collection, which began with the catalyst of "Bloom," she wrote to me, "I want to collect more moving and inspiring stories, to allow myself the financial and spiritual 'room' to be inspired by whatever is necessary in order to make this collection a group of poems that resonates with readers, that makes them feel connected to their deepest selves and to the world around us." As the book evolved, "Becoming the Blue Heron," the last poem in the collection, embraced this mission, drawing us into the movement and body of the heron with the second-person pronoun "you." In "Becoming the Blue Heron," this "you" fuses the heron and the human to become one, released in flight, shedding skin, free. *Becoming the Blue Heron* is a journey of a soul both grounded and in sync with the heavens, and everything in between.

Felicia Mitchell, Ph.D.
Emory & Henry College
November, 2016

Creativity is the Blue Heron within us waiting to fly;
through her imagination, all things become possible.

—Nadia Janice Brown

I

Lightning Bugs

Lightning bugs—little sparks from the earth's
fiery core, dusk's tiny lanterns—by their light,
I can see my childhood. I run barefoot again
through new-mown grass, my hair wild and

tangled as old fishing nets, the bulbs on those
blinking bodies leading us into our neighbors'
yards and down the sidewalk to the tune

of the streetlights' hum. Parents sit in semi-
circles on one another's front lawns, drinking
lemonade from Dixie cups and the occasional

Tom Collins until it grows dark and the time
comes to call their children in for baths and bed.
Then glass jars filled with dozens of flickering
bugs will flash yellow and green from night-

stands in a neighborhood where we fall asleep
in seconds, believing summer days will always
end like this one—our skin still glowing from
all the light we have gathered in our hands.

Sheller

for Mary Ann Eskridge

Though her skin has turned to rice paper,
her breathing shallow and sometimes labored,
she climbs the weathered stairs and crosses
the long boardwalk that leads to sand and sea.
At her back, the old lighthouse rises from the grassy
ground surrounding the Coast Guard station,
emitting every ten seconds, four one-second flashes
of light. And scattered across the dunes, sea oats
bob their blades to the crash of waves
while gulls wheel and cry above the sheller's bowed
head, her slight frame covered by a coat so heavy
she staggers at first beneath its weight.
Yet she keeps going, buffeted left and right
by a chill wind, winding her way to where a thin
layer of shells—angel wings and Scotch
bonnets, pen shells and olives—rests near the shoreline.
And some days, if she's lucky, she finds a whole
sand dollar with its Star of Bethlehem
pattern, the five doves hidden within this delicate
disk released only after the shell is broken,
but she will not break it. She will carry
it home in her pocket, picturing all the while
those unseen birds—their fragile wings spread
as if they are, already, in flight.

4

Pixie Cut

for my daughter

Black-eyed, black-haired girl of thirty-two,
I can see you reflected in a mirror
across the room—one of many mirrors and multiple stylists
with tattooed limbs and hennaed heads, clipping
and snipping. And I am thinking that the cloth draped
around your body, catching the sheared locks that tumble
to your shoulders, your lap, the floor, seems as sacred
as white linen on an altar table—your face emerging
like an angel sculpted from the clay
of your long, dark hair. You are smiling
because you see at last, what we all have seen—
how beautiful you are, that the woman you imagined
has arrived—
and she is, and always has been, you.

Twelve Dancing Princesses

There was a king who had twelve beautiful daughters. They slept in twelve beds all in one room and when they went to bed, the doors were shut and locked up. However, every morning their shoes were found to be quite worn through as if they had been danced in all night. Nobody could find out how it happened, or where the princesses had been. —The Brothers Grimm

Since growing older, the princesses prefer trains to boats.
They like the feel of flying above the tracks, how wooden
platforms, stepping on, stepping off, creak like the trapdoor
in their former bolted bedroom. After the King's death, they
never locked anything—not even their own houses, twelve
in a row, where each sister lives alone. The princesses enjoy
their privacy, but spend most evenings together as the eldest
is a widow and none of the others married. At home, they
wear yoga pants and sweaters instead of ball gowns, have
no use for dressing up when they go out. And because they
dance no more, they buy practical shoes that last for decades.
They feel no guilt about dead princes who chose their fate,
their faces blurring over the years like small print on menus.
Better to forget the men who lost their heads, failing to find
the dancers' palace. A poor soldier solved the puzzle and wed
the King's firstborn, becoming the heir to a sizeable kingdom
sold centuries later, to property developers. All towns need
a Walmart, or so the princesses were told. They miss those
nights of dancing, but with feet covered in calluses, corns,
and bunions, they frequent podiatrists now, rather than ball-
rooms. Still, the sisters seem content. They have each other
and immortality, thanks to a sorcerer's spell cast to thank their
father for a favor. He didn't tell the royal couple their dozen
daughters would age like everyone else, their ancient bodies
humming along forever, like Hondas. But the princesses' eyes
sparkle like leaves made of silver, gold, and diamonds. And
when they dream of tree-lined avenues, kettledrums and castles—
waltzing with handsome partners until their shoes are worn to
pieces, they wake up happy because their sisterhood is whole.

Spider in the Sink

Lighter than a breath, a spider speeds
across the silver sink—its belly lifted high
above its spindly, thread-thin
legs. It skitters across the slick surface
like a wind-driven skiff, between cups
and saucers, bits of eggs, a lone
blueberry, until it settles at last like a hand
tired from gesturing, settles into a lap—
the tiny flicker of its life like the faintest pulse
in the wrist of God, who made it.

Moon Walk

for my brother

Sunburned, bellies full of fried pompano, sweet
corn, and garden tomatoes purchased at a roadside
stand manned by a farmer with more fingers than
teeth—my family huddled around a rented black
and white TV set the shape and size of a two-slot
toaster, watching Neil Armstrong and Buzz Aldrin
hop like bunnies on the rough surface of the same
waxing moon that shone through our beach cottage
windows. I was eleven years old, bucktoothed and
long-legged—my brother a year younger and, most
days, followed his big sister like Mercury orbiting
the sun. Mom and Dad sat side by side on the faux
leather, sand-dusted couch, and Grandma, never one
to hold still for long, stood by her grandson's hard-
backed chair, her hair a nimbus of silver from the soft
glow of a television screen where a miracle unfolded
before our eyes. But grown men wearing fishbowls
on their heads, bouncing from one crater to the next,
seemed less real to my brother and me than Saturday
morning cartoons. And all the while, we could hear
waves slapping the surf and wind whipping across
the dunes—and the taste on every tongue was salt
and more salt. So when I picture the summer of '69
at Long Beach, North Carolina, as history rolled out
the red carpet leading to a future none of us could
foresee, my heart breaks like an egg against the rim
of what comes next. But let's pretend for the length
of this poem, that my brother's blood remains safe
inside his veins, Grandma's darkening mole as benign
as a monastery full of monks, and our parents, unable
to imagine the depth and breadth of grief. Here, there
is only goodness and mercy, the light of a million stars,
and the moon close enough now for anyone to touch.

Blue Jays

Bullies of the bird feeder, blue jays
blast their displeasure at smaller birds,
though most of them bolt

as soon as they see a flash of blue
feathers. They wait patiently on the limbs
of a dogwood tree—the yellow finches,

titmice, and Carolina wrens, for the blue
threat to pass, to take their long, sharp
beaks and petulant squawks

to another location, preferably miles away,
leaving scattered seed and empty husks
behind them, the same way

an inconsiderate guest eats more
than his share of hors d'oeuvres, grinding
crumbs into the carpet on his way out.

Valerie

My box-top baby doll, purchased with two dollars
and enough sugary cereal to propel
me to the moon and back, was no baby.
She had platinum-blonde hair set in waves
and wide-set blue eyes beneath a pair of arched,
painted-on eyebrows, her cheeks rouged
the same ruby-red that swirls around a peppermint
stick, with a red blouse to match. Her flared skirt
was edged in lace, and her shoes—white as whipped
cream—were a perfect fit for square feet
and fused-together plastic toes. But Valerie
seemed happy despite this disability,
as well as unbendable arms and legs, and a tiny
infantile nose. Maybe she was ignorant of the fact
that floating around the country were thousands
of copycat *Valeries* on their way
to (or already in the hands of) sugared-up little girls
of every shape, size, and description. And just think
how many *Valeries* were still at the Kellogg factory,
lying in cardboard boxes wrapped in cellophane—
their red, red lips smiling like our mothers
did in mid-afternoon, 1963, between blowing
smoke rings and staring into the distance
like they, too, were waiting for the mailman to deliver
a box-top doll that looked nothing like them, either.

Dragonfly

Chasing its mirrored image, a dragonfly skims
the surface of a lake—its iridescent body
shimmering with sunlight, wings beating faster
than a fetal heart. It weighs less than a flower
petal, yet dominates this idyllic scene, as present
and alive as the deer lowering their heads
to drink or the black bear lumbering
through the woods. Zigzagging across the water,
it fills the air with more sound than anything
so small should make—like a little boy playing
the tuba—then disappears faster
than a fighter jet, leaving behind a sonic
boom of silence.

Granny, Dragged by a Cow

In memory of my great-grandmother, Nannie White

When a hard, sinewy woman who has survived
the death of a son and the loss of three unborn
children is dragged across a field by her own cow,
it's tough to get past it, pride-wise. Folks couldn't
help but laugh at their stern-faced neighbor with
her foot stuck in Bessie's lead, her mouth open as
an unlatched gate, cheeks a violent shade of red.
But while Bess was pulling Granny like a plow,
her soul catapulted from her body like a stone
from a slingshot until she was riding sidesaddle
on her favorite quarter horse the way she used to
do before her daddy lost the farm and went to ruin.
Back then, her hair was so thick and difficult to
comb, her mother threatened to cut it with a hay
knife—nothing like the thin, gray braids coming
loose in the dirt old Bess was towing her through.
After that, Granny's spirit flew to her wedding
night, her handsome husband leaning in for a kiss.
And soon thereafter, she was rocking her baby
boy, staring into the bluest eyes she ever did see.
Come to think of it, she might have been close
to dying out there in that field, her ankle bound
by a rope and all the neighbors carrying on like
she was a freak show at the county fair. Or maybe
Granny's mind just needed a few minutes of free-
dom from a body tethered so tight to a world of
work and more work, not even a thousand pound
Holstein cow could drag her away from her hen-
raising, egg-gathering, butter-churning, biscuit-
making, bean-snapping, corn-shucking, supper-
cooking, Sunday-psalm-singing life for too long.

You

You will never drink moonlight
from my mouth, nor rest your
hand on my hip declaring, even
in sleep, *mine*. No breakfast table
for us, covered in bread crumbs
and newspapers—planning Sunday
and how to spend it, as if time
is cash money and we have won
the lottery. You will never see my
naked face, my bare feet. If you
sag from an unexpected punch,
the kind of pain that sends you
reeling, you will reach for someone
else, not me. Though I long for
you like penniless farm boys pine
for land—you are as lost to me
as my own childhood—a bright
red ball that flies again and again,
over a fence and out of sight.

Bloom

for Felicia

She is alone, save for the cat curled
around her feet, its fur thick as the winter
coat of a brown bear sleeping in its cave. The chill
wind roars through the woods like something dangerous—
yet tonight, she is warm and safe. Funny how cancer is silent,
like dark clouds floating over a field. Left unchecked,
it goes on doing its work—as if a body
is a house that needs tearing down, a place where no one wants to live
anymore. But she isn't done with her body, her life.
The ground may be frozen, but spring
will come again for her, the cat, the sleeping bears,
the birdsfoot violets, and the great blue heron
she saw last year along the Creeper Trail. The cup of tea
steaming in her hands will turn to lemonade
with shaved ice, and light will fall just so through the leaves,
the branches, calling to everything alive: bloom.

II

Carpenter Bee

Buzzing like a band saw,
a carpenter bee, its hard-shelled, blue-black
body glistening beneath the midday sun,

buries its head between the petals
of a tiny, purple flower. Its furry stole

is pollen-dusted, and a pair of wings,
patterned like stained glass
windows, are thrown behind its lacquered

back like the arms of a competitive swimmer
before the whistle blows. And as soon

as it flies away, a smaller bee takes its place
as if they are workers at the same
factory—one punching in, the other out.

Suppertime

In the narrow galley of her kitchen, my mother
stoops and lifts a wooden cutting board
from the cabinet that won't stay shut,
no matter how hard you close it. Somewhere
in the attic a lazy ghost grins, turns over
in his ghostly bed. So little work to do in an old
house, he thinks. It haunts itself.

She peels an onion, its glistening layers whiter
than the chipped sink they're landing in. A curl
escapes the thick coil of hair pinned
to the top of her head, so she pushes it back
with her wrist. She always was a beauty. Still
is, even in the harsh light that fans across
the cracked ceiling

and pools onto the tiled floor, the last project
my father tackled before life tackled him. He sits
in front of the TV, his chair pulled close
to the screen so he can see it. But the sound
of my mother moving between stove
and countertop, the clatter of pots and pans,
a paring knife knocking against

the cutting board is, for him, the sweetest music—
better than golf games or touchdowns. Soon,
she'll ask him to set up the folding trays
and he will do it. And as the sun climbs down
from its high horse and the moon readies
itself to hop on—they eat their supper,
the front door left wide open, lamps burning—

a sight so serene, if you happened to pass by
their house, you'd want to come in. So you watch
for a second or two, leash in hand, your dog
whining to move along—remembering a similar
scene from a movie someone you love
once starred in—maybe your own parents,
and some day, if you're lucky, you.

A Poem for Anders Carlson-Wee After Hearing Him Read His Work in His Publisher's Living Room

The son of Lutheran ministers, he knows how to rivet
a room, how to hold a book in his hands so it seems

like something he was born with, like fingers and toes.
It doesn't hurt that his eyes are the same color blue as

the vintage French coffeepot I found the other day. And
he's so young, you can't believe what he's done, already,

how rough at times, he chooses to live—hopping freight
trains, eating dinner out of dumpsters, trusting strangers

on the road who might covet the thing he carries inside
him—known by many names, but made of light. He is

every mother's son, the one who left and the one who
returned, clothes dusty, the soles of his shoes worn clean

through, with so many stories to tell, he could talk all
night, his words swooping through the air like starlings.

Zydeco

At Richard's Club in Lawtell, Louisiana,
seven miles from Opelousas, Boozoo Chavis
sings "Paper in My Shoe" to a packed room.
Sweat soaks the band of his cowboy hat and
pours from that fireplug body of his like water
off a chilled glass. Men grab their women and
vice versa, moving to music that slaves once
foot-stomped and hand-clapped after working
all day in the fields—accompanied tonight
by spoon-rubbed boards of corrugated metal,
guitars, electric bass, drums, and Boozoo's
accordion resting against his lemon-yellow
shirt and clear plastic apron he always wears
to keep his instrument dry. And the whole time
he's singing and playing, those jean-clad couples
keep turning around and around in a subtle lead
and follow, tension-producing, weight-shifting,
hip-centered zydeco style of dancing until the
floorboards glow like embers and grandmas and
grandpas tap their feet and sing along in Creole
patois as if English is their second language. Then
Boozoo slips into "Who Stole My Monkey" and after
that, "Sassy One-Step," until there's nobody we don't
love and no pain too heavy for any of us to bear.

Merlot Redbud

Covered in plum-
colored hearts,

the Merlot Redbud
gathers sunlight

and moonlight,
allows the wind

to have its way
with each wine-

stained leaf that
trembles, as my

body sometimes
will when I think

of you, then settles
into stillness—

like a feather lies
still after falling.

Monteen

Monteen's hair was bleach-blonde, her clothes
too tight. She left lights on and windows open.
When teenage boys hid in the bushes around her
house, she blew them kisses with her lipstick
slathered mouth that looked nothing like the thin,
red lines on their mothers' faces. Monteen's lips
reminded them of a movie star's pout, except
familiar, perhaps possible to kiss. But Monteen
kissed no one—not since her husband jumped
into his 1959 powder-blue Rambler and left her
for a barfly he met down at the pool hall who
knew *how to love a man right*. The pain of Jack's
departure was harder to bear than memories of
the fat bellies and beer breath of her stepfather's
poker buddies, who snuck down the hallway to
her bedroom until she borrowed her brother's
baseball bat and whacked a few heads with it—
one of whom still had a wonky eyeball from the
blow, the lousy bastard. Nobody messed with
her after that, not even her stepfather, the worst
of the bunch. At any rate, not much mattered to
Monteen after Jack left town, past, present, or
future. So she put on a show sometimes for the
local boys, just for kicks, and pretended not to
care that none of the wives in the neighborhood
so much as glanced in her direction. Husbands
did, however, and a few had the nerve to knock
on her door late at night, but she never answered.
They weren't young and fine like Jack with his
dark heavy-lidded eyes and black hair, the tattoo
of an eagle on his left bicep. But the man had no
mercy in him, and once a thing was over, he didn't

look back. She remembered being happy until
Jack grew bored and nothing she did was good
enough. He backhanded her once, leaving a sickle-
shaped scar on her cheek from his high school
ring—the only flaw on her otherwise perfect face.
But knowing Jack didn't care if she lived or died
was the burden she couldn't put down—her love
for him like two-sided tape, stuck to everything.

Black Vultures

A family business, handed down for generations,
black vultures are the undertakers
of the outdoors. A quiet bunch, they look so alike,

they might have been manufactured in a vulture
factory, their heads like a chain mail hood, bodies
fitted with the darkest

of suits. They can spot a dead deer from Pluto,
clean a carcass before it has time to fall. Defenseless,
save for making meals into missiles

and the stench from droppings drying on their legs,
they perform a job few other creatures would
want to do, full-time. And when

their work is done, they roost en masse on the bare
limbs of dead trees, preferring, even
in sleep, the feel of death beneath their flat feet.

Rail Walking

My great-grandfather liked to walk beside the railroad tracks early of a morning, no matter what the weather. He wore an old straw hat and overalls, his shoes thick-soled, stained with mud and whatever else he'd gotten into since the last time he cleaned them. He enjoyed the songs of white throated sparrows, the cardinals that called to one another from the shagbark hickories and pin oaks that grew along the tracks—and the whistle of a train coming or going. Either way, Papa wasn't on it. Maybe he wanted to be, but never said so. He spent his days building wooden coffins for a casket company, nights listening to Granny read from the Bible. Some-times they'd sing their favorite hymns without music, which is how they did things in the Primitive Baptist Church where he was an elder. But he heard the voice of God more often in quiet times alone, saw Him in the blue star and phlox, lyre-leaved sage and jack-in-the-pulpit. And however far he wandered and all the miles he traveled to find his way home, there was such kind-ness in his face and gentleness in his open hands that squirrels leaped from the tree branches to settle on his shoulders, and king snakes crawled across his path like he was part of the woods and fields and rocks and every natural thing they knew. Because my Papa's spirit was so pure and bright, he looked like a railroad lantern moving along the tracks. Wherever he walked, there was light.

Five Does

Emerging from the mist like mythical beasts,
five does dance across a rural road, hooves clicking
like tap shoes on the wet pavement. Tails

twitching, they leap over a ditch and into a patch
of dark woods that part like pine-patterned curtains.

Then the sun crests the tall trees like the sudden
switching-on of house lights after a Broadway show—

and the trampled weeds lift from the ground the way
theater patrons, still enchanted by a performance,
rise slowly from their seats after the play is done.

Pilar Rioja Dancing
in Neil Goldberg's Studio

*... I've always felt a contrast between the emotional
aspirations of my work and the unassuming place
where it's made. To illuminate that tension, I decided
to stage a larger-than-life performance by flamenco
dance legend Pilar Rioja and her company in my
300 square foot space.* –Neil Goldberg

Pilar Rioja waits, her face in profile
against a wide window—her lithe,
lean form drenched with light. Her
hand taps the sinewy muscles of her
black-clad thigh before she glides
to the center of the room, pausing
like a heron before it dips its beak
in water. And then she is water
and after that, the fish thrashing
through it. The sheer fabric of her
blouse caresses shoulders, arms,
and breasts, while the musicians
strum guitars and a man moans
rather than sings the words of his
song. Eyes wild, Rioja pummels
the floor as her lungs expand and
contract—expelling breaths both
guttural and erotic as cameras roll,
capturing on film one woman's
hot heart beating the ribcage of
a room far too small to contain it.
Yet, the walls hold and the dance
goes on—Rioja's heels pounding
death's unyielding chest like the
fists of a lover, betrayed.

Murmuration

Coordinating every movement with their seven
nearest neighbors, starlings flying

in flocks flee pursuing predators not as thousands
of singular birds, but as one shape-

shifting body that twists and turns, sometimes
spiraling into an hour glass that forms and un-forms

with such synchronicity and singleness of purpose,
perhaps even the falcon forgets

its gnawing hunger, laments for a second or two,
its life of solitude.

After the Explosion

for Tommy, 1959 – 1980

My brother, splayed on the concrete like a bearskin
rug, body broken, eyes filmy, died in a river of red
that flowed as if the summer air were a vampire
crazed with hunger. It ran in rivulets down the drive-
way, into a street lined with neighbors upon whose
retinas the image of his death was burned. Perhaps
his spirit lingered for a while, leery of its new and
borderless dimensions—entered a tool lying on the
garage floor, marveling at the chill of his cold, metal
skin. Next, the bee flying over the heads of paramedics
frantically working, the buzz like nothing he ever felt,
a rumbling deep in his chest, the clap of wings much
softer than hands. And after that, a few more stops—
the cement statue of the shy girl our mother bought
for the garden, the dog next door that wouldn't stop
barking, the taste of its pink tongue strange and wild
in a mouth that opened wider than any door. And out
of that dog's mouth my brother shot into the sky like
a bottle rocket, though none of us looked up. How I
wish we could have seen his swift ascent, the pressures
of his life: go to school, get a job, conform, conform,
conform—lift like a piano from his chest, his soul
rising weightless, without impediment, until he reached
the stars from which we all are made and zoomed by
them, faster than any plane he dreamed as a boy, to fly.

III

Rooster

Pride made flesh, the rooster struts his flashy,
feathered body, festive as a piñata, across the barnyard.

One might assume, from observing this bold
wattle-wobbling, head-bobbing stroll, that the pinnacle

of performance poultry has been achieved. But this
fine specimen of God's fertile imagination

has more in store for lucky listeners, particularly first
thing on a Saturday morning when his commanding

crow alerts every creature in close proximity
to the coop and possibly distant galaxies, that a new

day has arrived and roosters, rivaling the sun in their
magnificence, were designed to tell us so.

At the Bakery

Look at all the cupcakes lined up beneath
the counter, wisely kept behind a thick sheet
of slightly smudged glass or else the baby gazing
at them from her stroller would reach out
and grab one the way I want to do right now.
And placed just so beside them, are creamy éclairs
and miniature chess pies, pink lemonade squares,
and a coconut cake missing two slices. They say sugar
is bad for us but those sweet treats speak
to me like spurned lovers begging for a chance
to show me what I've been missing. What I'm really
missing, however, is the chocolate pound cake my Grandma
used to make for my birthday and, in fact, my Grandma,
herself, who spent endless hours cooking and baking
in the hot kitchen of her four-room house—
her apron, dusted with flour and powdered sugar, pulled
tight across a less-than-slim body made for hugging
and lap sitting, both of which I could use
at the moment. But since they don't sell chocolate pound
cake here and it wouldn't taste the same if they did,
I buy a red velvet cupcake and eat the whole
thing while sitting on a bench outside the shop.
And after I'm done, I crumple the brightly colored,
crumb-crusted paper and toss it into the trash, thinking
no matter how good it tastes, there's not enough sugar
in the world to fill the empty places left
by the people we love most and have,
for whatever reason, lost.

Pearl

Luminous as a lantern, Pearl's face glowed
in the lavender light of dusk, her laugh
tinkling across the yard like bells tied
to a baby's first shoes. Half-sister Nannie,
wed late and aging early, watched from
the shadows, a faded, floral dress tight
across her rump, calloused hands clenched.
Even Nannie's preacher husband, married
first to God, couldn't keep his eyes off
Pearl—made sure they served her cake
with clotted cream and fresh-milled coffee.
For years, Nannie's wrinkled chin quivered
with resentment, the taste in her mouth
bitter as bile until Pearl, her body butchered
by a surgeon's knife, walleyed and incoherent,
lay dying—though her face, lit from within
by some miracle of light, still shone.

Rosemary, Riding

*for Malaika King Albrecht and the Rocking Horse
Ranch Therapeutic Riding Program*

Out of the nostrils of God's innocent beast
comes the sweet scent of clover and tiny puffs
of pollen from a bee's jacket. And resting

on this creature's curved back is the saddle
that holds the child who cannot be touched
by human hands without cringing, but bends

low over the mane of her mount and croons
a song that must have been sung by the Creator
on the day He drew His plans for horses. And

with His arms outstretched, He brought them
forth from the nothingness of *before* and they
galloped and galloped through time and space

until they found this little girl and all the others
who called to them from birth—a kind of music
that only God and children and horses can hear.

Nostalgia

The past is a set of white curtains, a window
nailed shut beyond which everyone

is happy. There is no death, no disillusionment.
No one is sick. My parents' faces

are filled with light, as if their minds are made
of birthday candles, never blown out.

Who could wish for more than what they have,
already? I can see clearly, the perfect

body of my childhood—the girl with black hair
who runs and jumps with ease,

to whom pain means nothing more than skinned
knees or a baby tooth pulled from our mouths

by a string. And look at all the people—
aunts and uncles, grandparents, cousins, friends

and neighbors—my little brother trailing his big
sister like a tracker. And there is the house

I loved—glider on the front porch, swings in the
back—the kitchen table surrounded

by yellow chairs that seem so close, I can almost
touch them. Yet, the glass remains cold,

unyielding, impossible to shatter, the curtains
a pair of specters haunting the same small space.

Roofers

for Mr. Speaks

Soaked with sweat, t-shirts striped with dirt
and grit, they carry sacks of shingles
up the ladder to the roof. The day is boiling
hot, the sort of heat that saps

our strength, wrings from blistering bodies
every ounce of fluid. Yet these men toil
from *can't see* to *can't see*—until the slick
earth slips from the sun's grasp

into the cooling twilight. And while they work,
they live in a world with edges, each roof
like a map drawn by ancient cartographers.
But roofers are sure-footed and fearless,

their rubber-soled shoes heavy as hooves.
And when we look up, they seem as far above
the earth as constellations, light years away
from the sun-baked ground.

Four Finches and a Star

In the midst of a cold rain, four finches found
the Moravian star hanging from our porch,
each perching on a point. Swaying in the wind,

the star rocked those little birds for the length of
the storm, like babies sharing the same bassinet.
They didn't preen or sing or fight, but waited

with wings folded against their feathered flanks.
And when the rain stopped the finches flew, one
by one, like hands part after the prayer is done.

In the ICU

for Brandon

The man my daughter loves is sleeping,
his breath moving in and out

of his lungs, his lips curving into a smile.
He is tethered to the bed

by leads and tubes, like a boat securely
docked during a storm. Perhaps he

is dreaming of a vast lake, the two
of them swans, mated for life. They face

each other, floating—make the shape of
a heart with their long, white necks.

Old Photograph

In White Sands, New Mexico, the ground
is naked—its pale, granular skin
revealed. The wind has peeled it like a pear

that has long since dried out. The ghost
of water howls. White moths flutter bone-
white wings above white

lizards, white scorpions—the sand wolf
spiders with pallid legs splayed

like points on a star. Amid this blinding
whiteness, our brown-skinned
mother kneels. She holds her children

close. Already her son's spirit drifts, turns
away from the camera. We pose

on grains of gypsum that look like salt—
perhaps the dried tears of the milky
moon, a sky-mother who knows before we

do, what will happen—how a child's death
changes everything, how wind moves
dunes from here to there, then back again.

Angel

I used to see them walking, a middle-aged
man and his grown son, both wearing brown
trousers and white shirts like boys in a club,
or guys who like to simplify. But anyone
could see the son would never be a man who
walked without a hand to hold, a voice telling
him what to do. So the father held his son's
hand and whispered whatever it was the boy
needed to know, in tones so soft and low it
might have been the sound of wings pressing
together again and again. Maybe it was that
sound, since the father had the look of an angel
about him, or what we imagine angels should
be—a bit solemn-faced, with eyes that view
the world through a lens of kindness—who
sees every man's son as beautiful and whole.

Red and White Tulip

From its patch of dirt and mulch, my favorite
flower opens like a child's arms, welcoming

the morning sun, the sapphire sky. Milk-white
with ruby stripes, this tulip is the loveliest of

the lot, far outshining its purple neighbors.
It's petals part like the pages of an old book,

as if there is something written there, a secret
revealed, a poem or a prayer, a few words

from God. But there is no message—just its
soft center, tender as newborn skin, vivid as

a barber pole without the constant whirling.
Only a breeze or a breath moves it—leaves

and stem stirring, bulb bobbing, its pepper-
mint pores taking in the warm spring air.

Taharah

Part fish, part grieving widow,
I swim in the sea for hours.
Saltwater buoys my body far
beyond the breakers, though
I sometimes choose to brave
the waves. The large ones
drag me down with shards
of shells, blades of seaweed,
swirls of sand—leaving me
battered and beached. Others
bear my body to shore like
men who carry their lovers
to bed, except I am no one's
lover now. Remember our
first kiss, how my breastbone
broke and my ribs fanned
out, revealing the small red
bird of my heart? You drank
my tears of joy like a salt-
seeking moth. But you would
drown in them today, my love.
There are too many—the taste
of sadness, bitter on the tongue.
So I will soak my sorrow in
the sea, wrap it like a pure
linen shroud around an old
woman's flesh, washed clean.

IV

Barn Owl

Cordoned off and tethered to a stand, a barn owl
missing part of its wing stares at children,
teens and toddlers, parents and grandparents—
the whole crowd pressing against the rope, eager
to dive into a pair of black eyes so deep

and dark there could be blind fish swimming
in those caverns—stalactites
and stalagmites, the antithesis of light.

Yet, its tastefully earth-toned feathers look soft
as brush strokes, its face heart-shaped.

But let's call it what it is: the final Valentine
for rodents, certain death for bats that dart

too slow, the occasional rabbit caught in a clearing.
It hears the twitch of a whisker, a rustle
in the leaves. It floated once, over woods and fields

like a great gray ghost, the shock of its strike
a deadly blow—beak and talons tearing—
the echoes of squeals and shrieks still bouncing
from wall to wall of the barn owl's
tender, tufted throat.

Spring Rain

When mist rises from the wet ground
after an early-morning

rain, deer run through our backyards
like children

who have no boundaries when they
play. For a short time,

the day belongs to them—the world
so silent we can hear

their hoof beats—the moist air fragrant
with the sweet breath of fawns.

Washing Dishes

Side by side my parents stand at the old double
sink, doing the dishes from their supper. You
can see them through the kitchen window, Mom
washing, Dad drying, their faces glowing like
incandescent bulbs. My mother dips a dirty glass
in the warm, sudsy water, soaps it clean, and rinses
it off. Then she passes it to my father, who has
so little feeling in his knotty fingers a glass could
be a bubble for all he knows. Still, he manages
to hold it. He rubs its slippery surface with the
dishcloth and sets it in the drainer, then reaches
for a dinner plate and does the same. One by one,
they wash and dry them, every glass and plate
and bowl and pot until the counter is bare, all the
while talking the way people do when they've
known each other so long you'd think there was
nothing left to say. Yet for them, conversation
never ends. It is the music of my childhood, my
parents' voices—a comforting cadence to anyone
close enough to hear them sing to one another
night after night, their sweet dishwashing song.

Miniature Horses

Far off in a field, miniature horses
graze. They snort and whinny

through their tiny, wet noses, lower
their little heads so they resemble

not so much regular-size horses
shrunken in the wash, but handles

on briefcases, waiting to be carried.
Yet, these creatures know nothing

about work. They're content eating
breakfast beneath a bucket of blue

sky and its thin clabber of clouds,
their nostrils filled with the smell

of their own animal flesh and hot
manure, mixed with honeysuckle

and fresh-mown hay. Barely bigger
than a border collie, they've found

the key to contentment: Live in
the moment. In the moment, live.

Antiques

Two men toured an antique shop, one old,
the other older. Gray, grizzled,
and sporting ball caps, they wound their way
around the musty room, examining some things,
ignoring the rest. They didn't care for vintage purses
or postcards from France, fake pearl earrings
or paintings of fruit. They liked radios and rusted
scales, crates that once held apples, a catcher's
mitt. Picking up one item after another, the older man
told stories about his life to the younger in a voice
so loud, you could tell he'd been the smallest child
at the dinner table, struggling to be heard. The other
nodded and grinned, but didn't say much except
for, *You don't say?* and, *Is that right?*
as they meandered through the store like ghosts,
marveling at all the things they'd left
behind and how much they still missed them.

Jacqueline with Flowers

Jacqueline Roque and Pablo Picasso

Lying across Picasso's snow-covered grave,
Jacqueline willed her limbs to take root

in this sacred ground, the heat of her body
seeping through earth and rock to reach

him. If only he could feel it, could see she
wore his favorite gown. All through the night,

she fell in and out of sleep, dreamed she
was posing for him again in some soft shaft

of light, her face emerging from his brush
like molten glass from a blower's pipe—

her long neck made longer still, her profile
sarcophagal beside a wall of blue-tinged roses.

Red Lion

Oh red-haired boy I did not love, with your pockmarked
face and barrel-chested body—you shucked me like an
ear of corn at the Red Lion bar in Booneville after the

patrons went home and it was your turn to close the place
down. I can't believe I let you do it but I cared nothing

for myself back then and even less for you, so what did
it matter? I remember how you spread a bar towel on

the beer-splattered rug to protect my bare skin—that you
whispered my name so many times, it sounded like a poem
you say out loud until you memorize all the words. And

afterward, when you buttoned my shirt and zipped my
jeans, your big, clumsy hands trembled like paint shakers.

At least you didn't tell me you loved me except maybe
you loved me a little because your bloodshot eyes in the

neon light of the *Budweiser* sign hanging over a row of
half-empty liquor bottles, held a jigger-full of something
close to tenderness that I can still, on a good day, feel.

The Cost of War

Like flocks of birds, children gather between
the burned-out buildings, the hollowed husks
of homes and schools and hospitals that rise
from the ground like rotting teeth in the mouths
of monsters. Nothing keeps them from coming—
not even bombs blooming in the distance like
blossoms made of dust and debris, fouling the
air and blotting out the sun. They find a stick,
a ball, a song that needs to be sung, a game in
the midst of wreckage and ruin, the echoes of
their laughter bouncing off the hardened hearts
of warmongers and power players—men and
women who will win and lose, again and again,
the same scorched earth beneath the children's
bare feet. But the little ones are learning even
now, who the leaders are, the followers, who
cries at the first blow, which child endures. The
dark shadow of adulthood falls early across their
dirt-streaked faces, their whippet-thin bodies—
because there is no such thing anymore as play.

Bank Fishing at Smith Lake

Nodding, an old man leaves his favorite chair
in the living room of his house, his aching
arthritic fingers, the eyes that failed him—

and goes bank fishing with his buddies. He
holds the rod steady, sees plainly the lake's

distant shore. He fishes with dough sold by
the bait shop because it works so well for
catching bass and catfish. But *be careful*, he

tells his friend, *taking a catfish off the hook*.
They carry a sting in their spiny fins, close

to how it feels when, after a brief nap, he
wakes into his eighty-year-old body, neck
stiff, his hands empty of everything but time.

Electricity

My husband calls the sun *free light* in comparison to the lights
he constantly turns out, often in rooms where I'm still
standing. At war with the electric company, he reminds me
of my father who, in particular, wanted my brother
and me to keep the refrigerator door closed

at all times. To contemplate the panorama of delectable
leftovers beneath the blazing light of a miniscule bulb
that, in his mind, ate up more electricity than stadium lights,
was a sin at our house when I was growing up. In fact,

it was a blatant violation of the eleventh commandment—
Thou shalt not waste electricity—found nowhere in the Bible,
but as my father often intimated, understood by all sentient
beings. But he never uses hair dryers, curling irons,

or electric rollers, which no doubt clouds his perceptions
and my husband's, too, when it comes to the lure
of electricity, how it draws us in with promises of perfect
hairdos, as well as gorgeously lit rooms where the glow
of our loved ones faces creates memories that can't be counted

in kilowatts. The only electrical exception for both father
and husband, two men who cringe at the sight of well-lit
leftovers, rooms in which the corners are visible past
sundown, hair dryers that run long enough to dry one's hair—

are the big-screen TVs in both our houses, which can
be seen, if anyone happened to be there to observe, from Mars—
the use of which, particularly during football season,
will keep every employee at the electric company well paid,
well fed, and bi-annually vacationed into perpetuity.

Fund Drive

She could be a Norman Rockwell painting,
the small girl on my front porch with her eager
face, her wind-burned cheeks red as cherries.
Her father waits by the curb, ready to rescue
his child should danger threaten, his shadow
reaching halfway across the yard. I take the
booklet from the girl's outstretched hand,
peruse the color photos of candy bars and
caramel-coated popcorn, pretend to read it.
I have no use for what she's selling, but I
can count the freckles on her nose, the scars
like fat worms on knobby knees that ought
to be covered on a cold day like this, when
the wind is blowing and the trees are losing
their grip on the last of their leaves. *I'll take
two of these and one of those,* I say, pointing,
thinking I won't eat them, but I probably will.
It's worth the coming calories to see her joy,
how hard she works to spell my name right,
taking down my *information.* Then she turns
and gives a thumbs-up sign to her father, who
grins like an outfielder to whom the ball has
finally come—his heart like a glove, opening.

Family Album

Six years after my brother's death,
I took this beach trip
photograph. My mother,
resplendent in her black maillot,

sits on a towel beside my daughter,
who wears a bright red
bathing suit

with white polka-dots,
a fluted ruffle flaring above her plump,
three-year old thigh. Patterns
formed by shoe prints and crab

feet, dog paws and bucket rims,
surround them in the sand,
while waves, captured in mid-crash,
curl in the distance.

My child, half-turned, squinting
in the sun, flashes a mouthful of perfect
baby teeth. She clasps

her chubby hands, sticky with salt
and grit, as my mother smiles,
the sorrow in her eyes like blackened
wicks, smoking.

V

Ardea Herodias

The great blue
heron, caught by
my camera just as
its wings unfurled,
was only seconds
ago standing in the
shallow water of
a woodland trickle
like a monarch on
stilts, surveying
his kingdom. Its
bill, sharp as an ice
pick, was poised
to pierce a passing
fish or frog. Instead,
it cocked its head
as though listening
for a whisper, then
lifted its hollow-
boned body like
a practiced pilot.
It glided over leaf-
clogged rivulets,
clusters of rotting
reeds, the branches
of a black oak tree,
until blue sky and
bird mixed together
like paint—and the
heron was gone.

Caballero

Cowboy of my dreams, the man who rode
all day to get here: put your pistols down,
your hat anyplace but on the bed because
hats on a bed, my granny said, are bad luck.
Take off your dusty boots, your *chaperejos*.
Hang up your oil-skin coat. It is time for you
to rest. The cattle, all delivered—not one
calf lost. Your chores, all done. You have
doused the campfire, cleaned the skillet.
Your silver cup is tucked inside your saddle
bag, *la reata* coiled and ready to reel in the
next stray. I promise, you are safe. No bullet
will find you. No fist will meet your mouth,
moist from kisses. *Caballero de mis sueños,*
let my body be water. There is nothing for
you to do here, but cup your hands and drink.

Camellia

The camellia
bush

breathes
in chill winter

air—exhales
flowers.

The Street Walker

La Casque d'Or (Golden Helmet) and Toulouse-Lautrec

Imagine her surprise when Toulouse-Lautrec, son of first
cousins, barely five feet tall—wanted to paint a prostitute
in broad daylight and asked her to pose for him. Of all the
things men demanded of *La Casque d'Or*—this painter's

polite request for her to pose fully clothed in a Montmartre
garden, was the strangest. How absurd that this funny little
artiste with his stubby limbs and paint-flecked spectacles,

wanted to capture her face and form on canvas. Yet, she
did it—sat still and silent as bread on a plate while his gaze

roved over her figure without lust or judgment, but admiration,
even tenderness. And for years afterward, when her body
ached from the ill use of some overzealous lout, *La Casque*

d'Or would close her eyes, relive again and again the moment
she stood staring at the image of herself rendered by an artist
who found, beneath her yellow wig and rice-powdered skin,
the flicker of light left in her world-weary soul, and painted it.

Playing the Slots

for Maureen

A middle-aged man, who must be her son,
pushes an old woman in a wheelchair across
a carpet of crushed dreams. The casino air
is thick with heavy sighs and swirls of smoke
from a thousand cigarettes lit like campfires in
a canyon where loss howls from the hills like
hungry coyotes. The pair of them head toward
the slots with their neon faces and open mouths
begging for money, making promises that few
of them ever keep. But the man and his mother
don't speak. He seems to know which game she
wants to play or else chooses it for her the way
he chose her polyester pantsuit and slip-on shoes.
Pulling back the fake leather seat still warm from
the last player's disappointment, he moves her
wheelchair close to the machine and steps back
because she can take it from here. Her legs may
be weak but her hands still work and her purse
opens like all the rest. You can see how he might
have looked as a child standing by his mother
at the sink, watching her rinse a glass and place
it in the drainer just so, his eyes reflecting her
every move, his body so still he could have
been a pot waiting to be washed and put away—
how all too often, she forgot that he was there.

Frog Orgy

Pushing off the lake's sandy bottom,
hundreds of frogs propel themselves,
one toward the other—the males calling

and calling—vocal sacs like bubbles
blown beneath their chins in a frantic
search for partners. Once found,

they clasp the females' bodies, fertilize
eggs soon abandoned by every pair
of amphibious parents. No midnight

feedings, spit-up or diapers, no baby-
sitters or college funds for frogs. They
mate in the muck and part, their young

left for fish and birds to snack on. But
enough survive to turn into tadpoles
and finally adults desperate to follow

the ancient urge to make more and more
and more until the world is filled with
frogs—and still, they make more frogs.

Watching a Bald Eagle While
Eating Miss Charlotte's Apple Fudge
on the Back Porch at Altapass
Orchard

"See how the sun glints on her white
head?" said the white-haired man sitting
in a rocking chair

on the back porch at Altapass Orchard,
looking up. "That's a bald eagle.
Seen plenty of 'em in Alaska,

and she's a big one," he went on,
as the eagle stirred and stirred a bright
blue batter of sky.

COPD

Listening to my father cough, struggle for breath
when walking up a hill or climbing
the steep stairs to his bedroom, I want to lasso

the air, capture it like a runaway calf and give it
to him the way he used to bring home

money. Funny that air is plentiful and free,
yet he never has enough. Because my father's
lungs have turned against him like a friend will,

on occasion, without telling you the reason, he
wheezes, gasps, and sputters like an old

steam engine on its last lap around a lake. For my
father, I would rob a breeze-filled bank, empty

its vault of air and take the consequences. I dream
of cyclones, whirlwinds, Blue Northers, bull's
eye squalls, updrafts, downdrafts,

tornadoes, trade winds, mistrals, gales, williwaws,
and Nor'easters—so many ways for oxygen

to travel—then wake wondering why, when air
has such speedy transportation, my father
is forced to wait so long for a single sip.

Girl Riding a Bicycle,
Holding a Blue Umbrella

Somehow she managed it,
riding a bicycle while holding
an umbrella over her head,
a loaded backpack sagging
from the twin blades of her
slight shoulders. Like a moth
fluttering over a busy highway,
she seemed oblivious to danger,
that any moment she might be
broken. Cars flew by, flicking
her face with rainwater from
the road. A cold wind wrestled
with her umbrella, trying its
best to loosen her grip on the
handle. Still, she kept going,
her trajectory straight as a rock
flung into space by a slingshot—
legs pumping, umbrella like the
bowed back of blue sky made
solid—protecting her, as well
as any of us could, from harm.

Gulls

Swooping past the *Big Lots* sign
toward the Tractor Supply Store, a lone seagull flaps
what used to be white wings, dirtied now

by sludge-water and oil leaked from some good ole
boy's monster truck, and lands in the parking lot

among its peers. How these dozen or so gulls
got here, perhaps none of them remembers.
But they were born by the sea and somehow swept

miles inland to this patch of pavement outside
the place where farmers get everything they need,
save rain, and is always crowded. The air is filthy

from exhaust fumes and the tobacco-soaked sighs
of middle-aged men with thick bellies and vein-
roped arms, hoisting yet another sack

of seed across their meaty shoulders—the stench
of dumpsters and cigarette butts and dried sweat
more pungent as the day wears on—waves of heat

drifting over the pavement like steam from boiling
cauldrons, only hotter. On feet so fried they can't feel
them, the gulls feed on pieces of hotdog spewed

from the mouths of toddlers, covered with mustard
and phlegm, bits of stale bread hanging on
like pinchers. Whatever these birds knew of sea

and sand has been lost, yet they wheel and cry out
as if the sound still echoes over water, and any

minute a fish will leap from the blistering, trash-
strewn blacktop and cars will rise and fall
like shrimp boats riding the tar-tinted waves.

The Abortion

No woman has an abortion for fun. —Elizabeth Joan Smith

You could die, the doctor said, *if you have this baby* and death
Held no appeal. So I let them hoist my pregnant teenage body

Onto a cold table like a tenderloin that needed cleaving. And
Behold, I was delivered of a fetus whose sex I will never

Know while my legs shook the stirrups, the sound they made
Like rattling chains in a haunted house. *You should have*

Considered the consequences of your actions, said the multi-
Tasking medic vacuuming my uterus like a dirty rug—as if

A good scolding was what a girl like me deserved—the same
Girl who made straight A's in school and never gave her

Parents a moment's trouble. Yet my only child would never
Have been born save for the son or daughter sacrificed so I

Could go on living, this piece of past lodged in my memory
Like a splinter needled out now so forgiveness can find it.

The Day the Sun Became
a Woman

The day the sun became a woman,
she strolled through fields of tall
grass, touching the tips of every

stalk with golden hands. Her foot-
steps were silent. The bellies of birds
flying above her head flashed like

silver dollars tossed into the air, and
the wheat-colored grass gleamed.
But her yellow hair, her dazzling

dress, were dull compared to a face
from which all the light in the world
shone. Her radiance rippled across

the field and down the streets of the
nearest city and all the cities, entering
every human heart until weapons

fell from the hands of people who
held them and war became a word no
one knew, like darkness, like pain.

VI

IV

When Honey Bees Were Everywhere

Once, honey bees covered the clover-carpeted
ground, their steady hum linked so closely

with the clovers' heavy heads and thread-like
stems it could have been, instead, the language

of these fragrant flowers—perhaps what they
whispered to one another in the early morning

light on a summer day as the barefoot children
burst from their houses and the dogs began

to bark and the milkman with his big, brown
boots tromped through the yards, and mothers

dragged their laundry baskets across the grass
while bees scattered and the clover, briefly

trampled, rose again—their pale, dew-damp
faces poised to receive the bees' next kiss.

Dressing Room Blues

For one thing, there are never enough
hooks. And the lighting makes a mockery
of us all except teenagers who think they'll
look like that forever. And those Funhouse
mirrors add ten pounds to anyone's frame,
or so we tell ourselves as we tug and tug
the size we wore last year over this year's
body. And what about women who think
these stalls are soundproof booths? Some
cell phone conversations make you blush
when your face hasn't burned that bright
since menopause. But worst of all is trying
on the dress that called your name from
the rack—a garment that could have made
Mark Antony whistle and say to himself,
Cleopatra who? So you step into this dress
like holy water and it fits like it was made
for you by your own personal seamstress.
You're almost afraid to look because you
haven't found a mirror yet that can tell a lie—
but maybe this one will. Perhaps this beat-
up, quasi-distorted dressing room mirror
will somehow yield an image you can live
with. So you focus on the hemline, then
slowly lift your gaze, only to discover the
middle-aged woman who keeps filching
your reflection has stolen this dress, too.

Winter

Blooming with cardinals
and coated with ice, the slim
branches of a birch

tree sag, its trunk a frozen
sliver against the silvery sky.
Yet, the sun is creeping

over the hill, and a doe,
spindle-legged and shivering,
makes her way across

a field. Creaking like wooden
stairs, the stiff grass yields
to whatever moves

through it—the deer, a man's
heavy boots, the North
wind—spring.

My Father, Cutting
My Mother's Hair

When my half-blind father trims
my mother's hair,

he combs it first with fingers
so knurled and noduled it's hard

to hold the scissors. Still, he cuts
as best he can, a straight

line—the glossy
strands reflecting so much light,

even he can see them. So when
the gilded tips begin

to pool around his feet,
they seem to him like stars, newly

fallen. And his wife of sixty years,
her shoulders bare

above a towel—a vision no
invading darkness can ever steal.

Susan and Ray's

for Susan Nagel and Ray Bloch

At Susan and Ray's, guests sleep
on silk sheets. Through open windows
by the queen-sized bed, cool, crisp
air wafts through the screens. And not far
from the tree-lined street, a train rumbles
by on tracks that wind every-which-way
through the big city, but you don't mind it.
You like the lonesome sound it makes as you
slide across the slick mattress like a luge
on ice, your belly full of California rolls
and Graeter's mint chocolate chip.
And the sound of laughter from the bedroom
down the hall reminds you how it felt
to be a small child in your parents' house,
sung to sleep by muffled whispers and happy
sighs. You're safe here in this moon-dappled
mini-mansion with its dachshund-scuffed
hardwood floors and oriental carpets,
its comfortable couches and sturdy chairs.
And when morning comes, your room
is awash with the kind of light artists
travel miles to capture. There are scented
soaps and warm, hand-rolled towels,
breakfast on the patio with beloved friends.
Best of all is waking outside the wall
of your own well-built facade—
as if you've never been hurt or broken,
but born into a better world where
you are once again whole.

My Cousin, Milton

My cousin, Milton, worked for a cable company.
The boy I knew when we were children

had fists that were often clenched, his face set like
an old man whose life had been so hard,

it hardened him. But the man's hands opened to let
more of the world in. He sent the funniest

cards to family and friends at Christmas, laid down
cable so others could connect. Yet, he lived

alone, kept to himself much of the time, so when
his sister found his body, he'd been gone

a good while. He died young at fifty-seven, without
fuss or bother. No sitting by the bedside

or feeding him soup. He just laid himself down like
a trunk line and let the signal pass through.

Roller Skating

On winter mornings when it was too cold
to brave the outside world, we'd head
downstairs to the dank, musty basement,
fit our skates to our shoes, tighten the screws,
and take off rolling. Around and around
we went, past the washing machine
and dryer, the fat pipes connected to the clunky
old furnace, detritus from our father's
home improvement projects scattered over
the scarred tables and wooden benches that lined
the cinder block walls. My brother was shorter
and faster, but I was no less thrilled to feel
the soles of my feet tingle from the constant
motion of metal wheels against the oil-stained
floor where we skated for hours, passing
the earthy air back and forth as if we shared
one set of lungs between us, one
wildly beating heart.

The Gray and the Brown

All morning long the gray and the brown
lower their tapered heads, nibble

grass covered in mud from a recent rain.
It is warm for winter, but horses know

nothing of seasons save the sun
is a weightless rider and needs no saddle.

Come noon, they canter around the field
in tandem, carrying

nothing but light. Then they halt
like a horse and its shadow, motionless

as Paleolithic paintings in a cave—
a moment so fleeting and perfect, clouds

form in the shape of horses, gallop across
the sky in homage.

Downie Brothers Wild Animal Circus

My mother was too young to remember, so let's paint the scene
for her now, as vivid as the red circus trucks trimmed with silver
and gold that rolled through town in 1939. Picture her as a one-
year-old waving as the parade passes by, her auburn curls catching
the eye of a high-flying trapeze artist from the *Famous Morales*

Family. Listen to the calliope play, the shouts of children running
alongside it. Watch swirls of dust rise from the field next to my
grandparents' house, the pageant proceeding to the place where
they'll pitch the Big Top. Imagine the loveliest woman you'll ever
see, her smooth, muscular limbs, her sequined skirt—how she

knocks on my grandparents' door, asks to show their *pretty baby*
to friends at the circus—how she cradles my mother and marches
across the field, crooning. Picture my grandmother following close
behind them, trying to keep pace with an aerialist used to soaring
above the crowd, her body glinting like glass. You pass a pair of

zebras, then the elephants—Tena, Babe, Pinto, and Queen. There
are bears behind makeshift fences, two-hump camels, tigers, lions,
razorback hogs, and Professor John's high-jumping greyhounds.
See jugglers, wire-walkers, and clowns, bareback riders grooming
horses with feathered plumes springing from their foreheads. And

the searing summer air is pungent with the smell of popcorn, peanuts,
animal dung, and sweat. It's grueling work, setting up the Big Top—
a circus with wild animals, sideshows, grandstands, and concessions.
Tougher still, dismantling rings, tearing down tents, and leaving the
littered fields with kids crying *good-bye, good-bye*, the calliope silent.

Variegated Fritillary

for Ron Powers

Feeding on bearded beggarticks,
the variegated fritillary flutters its

checkered wings—pale orange with
wavy black lines and scalloped edges

on the outside, brown and tan on the
inside, resembling a dead leaf. When

flying, it looks like a mobile stained
glass window, as if the meadow has

become a church where we can all
worship the way it should be done—

lying flat in a field watching clouds
float by, while fritillaries land on our

fingertips and toes, mistaking us, if
we are still enough, for wildflowers.

The Oceanic

for Leonard

We are sitting at a table on the top floor of the Oceanic
where all of the views are good and we've just ordered
fried oysters, which I may regret later. But when the
waiter places the plate in front of me, it looks like the
sort of meal that might be served in heaven where there
are no concerns about cholesterol and nothing you can
eat is poison in the guise of culinary ecstasy. And while
we don't have much new to say to each other after twenty-
four years of marriage, the whirring fans on that clap-
board ceiling sound like flocks of wild geese flapping
their wings in flight. And through salt-crystaled panels
of glass, come the sound of waves crashing on the beach
and seagulls crying out like the beggars and scavengers
they are, yet sunlight flashing on their feathers is close
to blinding in its beauty. And the cutlery shines like cut
diamonds, the knife and fork weighty the way you'd think
a queen would require of her royal silver, only it isn't real
silver, but who cares? So what if you don't look at me with
the longing you felt before our first kiss when I hooked
my leg around yours and we stood in the doorway of my
apartment for at least a hundred years, lips locked and
hearts thudding like footsteps running toward something
incredible waiting around the corner if we could just get
there before it was gone. Your gaze, which has since high
school slid over my face like the sun rolling across the
sky, is familiar and comforting. And you are still hand-
some, I have to say, and I'm not half-bad, either, even if
sixty will, in a few more years, claim its due from my
aging body. We've still got it, haven't we, Darling? And
we'll keep it a while longer, as long as we can, as long as
there are days left like this one when nothing much hurts
us except, perhaps, that bothersome twinge in your lower

back and my propensity to think of each passing moment
as being all too brief and poignant—worth holding onto
even as the memory is being made because I can't seem
to hold tight enough to your hand nor to the time already
slipping away like the linen napkin falling to the floor as
I lean over to kiss your beloved, fried oyster-flavored lips.

Becoming the Blue Heron

In muddy water by a pile of poplar limbs, you
spot a great blue heron, bill pointed skyward.

Imagine you can fly. Imagine deciding, not in
words but in images of other flights, it is time

for you to go. But you are hungry and fish are
flickering through clouds of silt. So first you

feed, forgetting the woman who shed her skin
and stepped into a heron's blue body. It is your

body now. Feel the lightning thrust, how fish
slide down the chute of your S-shaped neck.

You have no way to describe it. But someone
will say her pulse quickened to the flap, flap of

your great blue wings as you ascended from the
shallows, a sound she hears clear across the lake,

though you won't see her. You fly past the place
where she is standing. You don't look down.

Acknowledgments and Notes

My deepest thanks to God for his healing grace and mercy, for all of the beauty in this world, for being the author of love, and for creating great blue herons and lightning bugs and horses and tulips and everything else that makes life worth living.

Special thanks to my beloved and gorgeous mother, Loretta Kirby, and to soul sister, poet, and educator Dr. Felicia Mitchell, for being the first readers of this manuscript (to Felicia for crafting a beautifully written *Introduction*, as well), and to my sweet "daddy," Tom Kirby, for not only being a wonderful father, but for listening as Mom reads my poems to him due to his limited vision.

Thanks, also, to my loving husband, Leonard Erickson, who genuinely thinks I look great with or without lipstick (!) and supports my writing life in every way, to my darling daughter, Gia, and her partner, Brandon, who makes her so happy, and to my uncle, artist Stephen White, whose exquisite paintings grace the covers of all of my books to date. My love always and forever to my late brother, Tommy, 1959 – 1980.

To dear friends Susan Nagel-Bloch, Harriet Strickland, Maureen Sherbondy, Maricam Kaleel, Tim Plowman, Frances Y. Dunn, Kathryn Milam, Mark C. Houston, Debra Hardiman, Mick Scott, Debbie Kincaid, Lou Ann Spell, Ron Powers, Anya Silver, Kitty Jordan, Malaika King Albrecht, Pete Fenninger, Nick Nicholas, Pamela Byrd, the "Susans," and a long list of other fine people whose friendship means the world to me—thank you, from my heart. And to Rolland Barrett, MD, thank you for decades of kindness and care in the lives of so many.

To brilliant writers Diana Pinckney and Ann Campanella, and award-winning journalist, CNN Executive Editor Arthur Brice—I so appreciate your kind words about this book. To friend and publisher, Kevin Morgan Watson of Press 53, thank you, thank you...into infinity. And finally, to you, dear readers, thank you for your support of poets and poetry!

It might be of interest to note that in August of 1939, the Downie Brothers Wild Animal Circus set up their tents in a field next to my grandparents' house in Winston-Salem. Interestingly, a man named James "Jimmie" Heron was, for a period of time, manager of this circus, which fits in nicely with the title of this collection!

For more information about (and how to donate to) Rocking Horse Ranch Therapeutic Riding Program in Greenville, NC, a not-for-profit organization that "provides equine assisted activities and equine assisted therapy to children and adults with a variety of physical, cognitive, and psychological disabilities," please visit www.rhrnc.com.

To donate to The Centers for Exceptional Children in Winston-Salem, NC, (where my middle school math teacher and friend, the late and much loved Mike Britt, was the executive director for many years), please visit www.thecfec.org. The good people at the CFEC, who have dedicated their lives to special needs children, truly see "every man's son (and daughter) as beautiful and whole."

Terri Kirby Erickson is the author of five full-length collections of award-winning poetry. Her work has appeared in the *2013 Poet's Market*, Ted Kooser's *American Life in Poetry, Asheville Poetry Review, Atlanta Review, Boston Literary Magazine, Christian Science Monitor, Cutthroat,* JAMA, *Literary Mama,* NASA *News & Notes, North Carolina Literary Review, storySouth, The Southern Poetry Anthology* (Texas Review Press), *The Writer's Almanac with Garrison Keillor, Verse Daily,* and many others. Awards include the Joy Harjo Poetry Prize, Nazim Hikmet Poetry Award, Atlanta Review International Publication Prize, Gold Medal in the Next Generation Indie Book Awards, and a Nautilus Silver Book Award. She lives in North Carolina.

STEPHEN WHITE specializes in figurative paintings done on wood in gold leaf and transparent oil glazes. His work is available through the Little Art Gallery in Raleigh, North Carolina, and Village Smith Gallery in Winston-Salem, North Carolina.

CPSIA information can be obtained
at www.ICGtesting.com
Printed in the USA
BVOW08s2105151017
497686BV00001B/2/P